# Slay Your Debt Dragon
## Your Step-by-Step Guide to Financial Freedom
### By John Nowinsky

(c) 2024 – John Nowinsky

All rights reserved. No part of this book may be reproduced or transmitted in any form or by any means without written permission from the author.

## Dedication

To my mom and dad who inspired me to be the man I have become.

To God who has reached out to me numerous times and said I have job for you and by accepting I have found my life go in directions I never would have imagined.

## About The Author

Hi, my name is John Nowinsky. Rather, than bore you with the details of my personal life.

I want to take a moment and share with you how I got to this place in my life.

I answered God's calling upon life to become a caregiver at a memory assisted living facility. Yes, I moved away from a career in computer and accounting but when you answer God's calling. Life takes on new meaning and fulfillment.

There is no greater pleasure than making a difference in the life of someone. That one on one connection is a blessing for me and the one I'm with at that moment.

God has now called on me to write these books so that I can continue helping to make a difference in the lives of others.

# Table Of Contents

| | |
|---|---|
| Introduction | 6 |
| **Part 1: Understanding Your Debt Monster** | 9 |
| Chapter 1: The Debt Dragon Awakens | 10 |
| Chapter 2 Cracking the Debt Code | 15 |
| **Part 2 Forge Your Debt-Slaying Strategy** | 20 |
| Chapter 3 Choose Your Weapon | 21 |
| Chapter 4 A Last Resort: Facing Financial Bankruptcy | 30 |
| Chapter 5 Negotiation Ninja: Conquering Credit Card Conversations | 35 |
| **Part 3 Prepare for Battle: Launching the Attack** | 40 |
| Chapter 6 Gear Up for Liftoff | 41 |

Chapter 7 Taking Flight: Contacting Your Credit Card Company — 46

Chapter 8 Striking a Deal: The Negotiation Arena — 51

Chapter 9 Facing the Debt Collectors — 57

**Part 4 Slay the Dragon: Sticking to Your Repayment Plan** — 69

Chapter 10 Building Momentum: Crafting Your Budget Weapon — 70

Chapter 11 Fan the Flames of Motivation — 78

**Part 5 Fortify Your Finances: Building a Secure Future** — 84

Chapter 12: Rebuild Your Credit Walls — 85

Chapter 13 Live Within Your Means: The Long-Term Defense — 88

**Conclusion Your Financial Freedom Starts Now** — 96

**Appendix Resources for Financial Empowerment** — 100

# Introduction

**Your guide to Conquering Debt**

I remember when my friend, Betty, came to me in tears, feeling overwhelmed by her credit card debt. She had accumulated $20,000 in debt after a series of unexpected medical bills and car repairs, and was struggling to make ends meet. Despite her best efforts, she felt like she was drowning in debt, with no clear way out. But together, we created a plan to tackle her debt, and within two years, she was debt-free.

As I reflected on Betty's journey, I realized that her story was not unique. In fact, credit card debt has become a staggering $1.5 trillion crisis in the United States alone, with the average household owing over $15,000. This burden can lead to stress, anxiety, and feelings of helplessness.

But there is hope. By facing your debt head-on and taking control of your financial situation, you can break free from the cycle of debt and start building a brighter financial future. In this book, we'll explore the strategies and mindset shifts necessary to overcome credit card debt, from debt consolidation to balance transfers, hardship programs, and debt settlement. We'll also tackle the emotional and psychological aspects of debt, helping you build a support system and stay motivated throughout your journey.

As you read this book, you'll learn how to:

**Create a personalized plan to tackle your debt**

**Negotiate with creditors and settle debts**

**Build a support system and stay motivated**

**Develop healthy financial habits for long-term success**

Are you ready to transform your financial future? Start your debt-free journey now by pouring yourself a cup of coffee and turning the page!

# Part 1: Understanding Your Debt Monster

# Chapter 1: The Debt Dragon Awakens

**Confronting Your Debt: Why It Matters and How to Start**

Are you tired of living in fear of your credit card debt? Do you avoid opening your statements or checking your balance because you're afraid of what you might see? You're not alone. Credit card debt can be a daunting and overwhelming monster, but it's time to face it head-on. In this chapter, we'll explore why confronting your debt is crucial, the negative consequences of ignoring it, and the benefits of tackling it. You'll also find exercises to help you acknowledge the total amount owed across all credit cards and create a plan to slay the debt dragon.

**Why Confront Your Debt Head-On?**

Ignoring your credit card debt won't make it disappear. In fact, it can lead to more harm than good. When you avoid confronting your debt, you're allowing it to control you. You're giving it power over your financial decisions, your stress levels, and your overall well-being. By facing your debt head-on, you're taking back control. You're saying, "I acknowledge you, debt, but I won't let you define me."

## Negative Consequences of Ignoring Your Debt

Ignoring your credit card debt can have severe consequences on your financial health and overall well-being. Some of the negative consequences include:

Impacted Credit Score: Missed payments, high balances, and ignored debt can significantly lower your credit score. This can make it harder to get approved for loans, apartments, and even jobs.

Increased Stress: Avoiding your debt can lead to increased stress and anxiety. You may feel like you're living in a constant state of financial uncertainty.

Potential Lawsuits: If you ignore your debt for too long, creditors may take legal action against you. This can result in wage garnishment, bank account seizures, and even bankruptcy.

Emotional Toll: Debt avoidance can lead to feelings of

overwhelm, anxiety, and depression. You may feel like you're drowning in debt with no escape.

### Benefits of Tackling Your Debt

On the other hand, tackling your debt can have numerous benefits, including:

Financial Freedom: Paying off your debt can give you the financial freedom to make choices that align with your values and goals.

Peace of Mind: Knowing that you're in control of your finances can give you peace of mind and reduce stress.

Improved Credit Score: Paying off your debt and making timely payments can significantly improve your credit score.

Increased Financial Flexibility: With reduced debt, you'll have more money to invest, save, or spend on things that matter to you.

### Exercises to Help You Acknowledge Your Debt

It's time to face your debt head-on. Take out a piece of paper and a pen, and follow these exercises:

**Write down the total amount owed across all credit cards.**

**List the interest rates and minimum payments for each card.**

**Calculate the total minimum payment due each month.**

**Write down how you feel about your debt.**

**Create a list of goals you want to achieve once you're debt-free.**

**Case Study: Sarah's Story**

Sarah, a graphic designer, realized her spending habits had gotten out of control after a series of unexpected medical bills landed on her credit cards. She ignored the debt, hoping it would magically disappear. But the debt only grew, and so did her stress and anxiety. Finally, she decided to face the dragon and take control of her finances. With the help of a credit counselor, Sarah created a budget, negotiated with her creditors, and started making payments. It wasn't easy, but she persisted. Today, Sarah is debt-free and has a newfound appreciation for financial freedom.

## Your Financial Freedom Starts Now

By acknowledging your debt, you've taken the first crucial step towards vanquishing it, just like Sarah. You've faced the dragon, and you're ready to take control. Remember, confronting your debt is the first step towards financial freedom.

## Deciphering Statements and Building Your Arsenal

In the next chapter, we'll explore how to obtain and review your credit card statements to gain a clear picture of your debt. You'll learn how to gather intel, create a budget, and start making payments. The journey ahead won't be easy, but with the right tools and mindset, you'll be able to slay the debt dragon and achieve financial peace.

# Chapter 2
# Cracking the Debt Code

**Become a Debt Detective Today!**

Welcome to the next step in your debt-slaying journey! In this chapter, we'll transform you into a debt detective, gathering crucial intel to understand your financial situation. By obtaining and reviewing your credit card statements, you'll uncover the secrets of your debt and gain a clear picture of the enemy you're up against. So, grab your magnifying glass and let's dive in!

**How to Obtain and Review Your Credit Card Statements**

The first step in cracking the debt code is to get your hands on your credit card statements. You can usually find them online by logging into your credit card account or by requesting a paper copy from your credit card issuer. Once you have them, take a deep breath and start reviewing!

Understanding Key Terms

As you scan your statements, you'll come across terms like

interest rates, minimum payments, annual fees, and late payment penalties. Don't worry if you're not familiar with these terms – we'll break them down for you:

**Interest Rates:** The percentage of your outstanding balance charged as interest. There are different types of interest rates, such as fixed and variable. Fixed interest rates remain the same over time, while variable interest rates can change.

**Minimum Payments:** The smallest amount you can pay each month without incurring penalties. Minimum payments are usually calculated as a percentage of your outstanding balance.

**Annual Fees:** Yearly charges for using the credit card. Some credit cards have no annual fees, while others charge a hefty amount.

**Late Payment Penalties:** Fees incurred when you miss a payment. These penalties can add up quickly, so make sure to pay your bills on time!

### Calculating the Total Amount You Owe

Add up the outstanding balances, interest accrued, and any fees to get the total amount you owe. For example:

Outstanding balance: $2,000

Interest accrued: $500

Annual fee: $100

Late payment penalty: $25

Total amount owed: $2,625

**Organizing Your Debt Information**

Use a spreadsheet or notebook to organize your debt information, including:

Credit card issuer

Outstanding balance

Interest rate

Minimum payment

Annual fee

Late payment penalty

You can also use a debt tracking template or worksheet to help you stay organized.

### Case Study: Michael's Mistake

Michael, a recent college graduate, wasn't familiar with credit card terms like interest rates and minimum payments. He ended up accumulating a significant amount of debt without realizing the true cost. By gathering intel on his statements, Michael understood the severity of his situation and could start formulating a plan.

"I was shocked when I saw how much interest I was paying," Michael said. "I had no idea it was so high. But once I understood the terms and calculated my total debt, I felt empowered to create a plan to pay it off."

### Putting Your Debt Knowledge into Action

Gaining a clear picture of your debt empowers you to make

informed decisions to defeat it, like Michael did when he reviewed his credit card statements. You now have the tools to understand your debt and create a plan to tackle it. Pat yourself on the back – you're one step closer to financial freedom!

## Exploring Tactics to Conquer Your Debt

With your debt information organized, you're ready to explore strategies for tackling your debt. In the next chapter, we'll discuss various approaches to debt repayment and help you choose the best weapon for your debt-slaying journey. Get ready to take action and start slashing that debt!

# Part 2
# Forge Your Debt-Slaying Strategy

# Chapter 3
# Choose Your Weapon

## Strategies to Manage and Eliminate Debt

Are you tired of feeling like you're drowning in credit card debt? Do you dream of achieving financial freedom and living a debt-free life? You're not alone! Millions of people struggle with credit card debt, regardless of the amount. The good news is that there are various strategies to help you slay the debt dragon and achieve financial freedom.

### Debt Consolidation: Combining Multiple Debts into One Loan

Debt consolidation involves combining multiple debts into one loan with a lower interest rate. This approach simplifies your repayment process, making it easier to manage your debt.

**Pros:**

Lower interest rate

Single monthly payment

Simplified repayment process

Reduced stress

Potential to save money on interest charges

**Cons:**

May not lower the total amount owed

Requires discipline to avoid accumulating new debt

May impact credit score if not managed properly

Some consolidation loans may have fees

**Types of Consolidation Loans:**

Personal loan

Home equity loan

Credit card consolidation loan

Student loan consolidation loan

**How to Choose the Right Consolidation Loan:**

Research and compare interest rates

Consider fees and repayment terms

Check your credit score and history

Consult with a financial advisor if needed

**Example:**

Sarah consolidated her three credit card debts into a single personal loan with a lower interest rate. She saved $200 on interest charges and simplified her repayment process.

**Balance Transfers: Moving Your Debt to a New Card**

Balance transfers involve moving your debt to a new credit card with a 0% introductory APR period. This approach can save you money on interest charges and help you pay off your debt faster.

**Pros:**

0% introductory APR period

Savings on interest charges

Opportunity to pay off debt faster

Potential to improve credit score

**Cons:**

Introductory period may expire

New credit card may have fees

Requires discipline to avoid accumulating new debt

May impact credit score if not managed properly

**How to Choose the Right Balance Transfer Credit Card:**

Research and compare introductory APR periods

Consider fees and repayment terms

Check your credit score and history

Consult with a financial advisor if needed

**Example:**

John transferred his credit card debt to a new card with a 0% introductory APR period. He saved $500 on interest charges and paid off his debt within the introductory period.

### Hardship Programs: Negotiating with Credit Card Companies

Hardship programs involve negotiating with credit card companies to lower interest rates or waive fees due to financial hardship. This approach can provide temporary relief and help you get back on track.

**Pros:**

Lower interest rates

Waived fees

Temporary relief

Potential to improve credit score

**Cons:**

May impact credit score

Requires proof of financial hardship

Limited duration

May not be available for all credit cards

**How to Negotiate with Credit Card Companies:**

Contact your credit card company's customer service

Explain your financial situation and hardship

Request a lower interest rate or fee waiver

Be prepared to provide financial documentation

**Example:**

Emily negotiated a hardship program with her credit card

company, reducing her interest rate and waiving fees. She was able to get back on track with her payments and improve her credit score.

## Debt Settlement: Negotiating a Lump-Sum Payment

Debt settlement involves negotiating a lump-sum payment to settle your debt for less than the total owed. This approach can provide a fresh start, but it may negatively impact your credit score.

**Pros:**

Fresh start

Reduced debt amount

Potential to save money

**Cons:**

Negative impact on credit score

May require a large upfront payment

Not suitable for all situations

May impact credit report

### How to Negotiate a Lump-Sum Payment:

Contact your credit card company's customer service

Explain your financial situation and inability to pay

Offer a lump-sum payment

Be prepared to provide financial documentation

### Example:

David negotiated a debt settlement with his credit card company, paying a lump sum of $2,000 to settle his $3,000 debt. He avoided bankruptcy and got a fresh start.

### Case Study: Lisa's Consolidation Choice

Lisa, a single mom, was struggling to keep up with payments on multiple high-interest credit cards. She decided to consolidate her debt into a single loan with a lower interest rate, simplifying her repayment process and saving money on interest in the long run.

## Tailoring Strategies to Your Goals

Each debt-slaying strategy has its advantages and disadvantages. It's essential to evaluate your situation and choose the approach that best aligns with your goals, like Lisa who opted for consolidation. Take your time, consider your options carefully, and remember that achieving financial freedom is within reach.

## Exploring the Option of Bankruptcy

Now that you've explored various debt-slaying strategies, it's essential to understand the last resort option: bankruptcy. While it may seem like a drastic measure, bankruptcy can provide a fresh financial start for those overwhelmed by debt. In the next chapter, we'll delve into the world of bankruptcy, exploring its different types, eligibility requirements, and legal and financial ramifications.

# Chapter 4
# A Last Resort: Facing Financial Bankruptcy

## Unveiling the Realities of Bankruptcy

When struggling with credit card debt, it's essential to explore all possible avenues before considering bankruptcy. While it may seem like a quick fix, bankruptcy has long-term consequences that can impact your financial future. However, for some, it may be the only viable option to escape the suffocating grip of debt. In this chapter, we'll delve into the world of bankruptcy, exploring its various forms, eligibility requirements, and the legal and financial ramifications of filing.

## Different Types of Bankruptcy and Eligibility Requirements

In the United States, there are several types of bankruptcy, each designed for specific situations and individuals. The most common forms of personal bankruptcy are Chapter 7 and Chapter 13.

**Chapter 7 Bankruptcy**: Also known as liquidation bankruptcy,

Chapter 7 involves the sale of non-exempt assets to pay off creditors. Eligibility requirements include:

Passing the means test, which determines whether your income is below the state median.

Not having filed for Chapter 7 bankruptcy in the past eight years.

**Chapter 13 Bankruptcy**: Also known as reorganization bankruptcy, Chapter 13 involves creating a repayment plan to settle debts over time. Eligibility requirements include:

Having a steady income.

Having debts below the allowed maximum (approximately $1.3 million in secured debt and $400,000 in unsecured debt).

**The Legal and Financial Ramifications of Filing for Bankruptcy**

Filing for bankruptcy can have significant legal and financial consequences, including:

**Automatic Stay**: A temporary halt on creditor collections, providing breathing room to reorganize finances.

**Discharge**: The elimination of qualifying debts, freeing you from payment obligations.

**Public Record**: Bankruptcy filings are public records, potentially affecting personal and professional relationships.

**Legal Fees**: The cost of hiring a bankruptcy attorney, which can vary depending on the complexity of the case.

## The Impact of Bankruptcy on Your Credit Score and Future Borrowing Ability

Bankruptcy can significantly impact your credit score, making it harder to secure loans or credit in the future. The effects of bankruptcy on your credit score can last for:

**Chapter 7 Bankruptcy**: Up to 10 years from the filing date.

**Chapter 13 Bankruptcy**: Up to 7 years from the filing date.

Case Study: David's Difficult Decision

David, a small business owner, was hit hard by an economic downturn. Despite his best efforts, his business debts became overwhelming. After exploring all other options, David decided filing for Chapter 7 bankruptcy was the only way to get a fresh financial start.

"I felt like I'd failed, but my attorney explained that bankruptcy was a tool to help me move forward. It wasn't easy, but it was the best decision for my business and personal well-being," David said.

## A Last Resort

Bankruptcy should be carefully considered, as it has long-term consequences, like in David's case. While it may provide a fresh start, it's essential to explore other options first, such as debt consolidation, credit counseling, or negotiating with creditors. Remember, bankruptcy is a last resort, but it can be a necessary step towards financial recovery.

## Negotiate Your Way to Financial Freedom

While bankruptcy may seem like a daunting option, it's crucial to understand its implications and potential benefits.

In the next chapter, we'll discuss how to negotiate with your credit card company and develop a plan to tackle your debt. By exploring all avenues and creating a personalized plan, you can take the first steps towards financial freedom.

# Chapter 5
# Negotiation Ninja: Conquering Credit Card Conversations

## Mastering Negotiation for Debt Relief

When facing credit card debt, it's essential to learn the art of negotiation to secure favorable deals with your credit card company. By mastering the skills of effective communication and using sample scripts as a guide, you can conquer the daunting task of negotiating with your creditors. In this chapter, we'll explore the power of clear communication, sample scripts, and additional tips to help you become a negotiation ninja.

## The Power of Clear Communication

Clear and concise communication is the foundation of successful negotiation. By being prepared and articulate, you can build trust and credibility with your credit card representative. Remember, the goal is to find a mutually beneficial solution, not to engage in a confrontation.

## Sample Scripts as Your Armor

Sample scripts provide a framework for your negotiation, boosting your confidence and helping you stay focused. Adapt these scripts to your specific situation, and don't be afraid to add your personal touch.

### Script 1: The Interest Rate Tango

**Opening**: "Thank you for taking the time to speak with me today. I'm experiencing financial hardship, but I've consistently made on-time payments in the past."

**Request**: "I'm asking for a specific interest rate reduction to 12% to help me continue making payments without defaulting."

**Closing**: "Thank you for considering my request. I'm committed to working together to find a solution."

### Script 2: The Fee Forgiveness Waltz

**Opening**: "I apologize for the recent late payment, which was due to an unexpected expense."

**Request**: "Considering my typically on-time payment history, I kindly request a waiver of the late fee."

**Closing**: "Thank you for your understanding. I'm committed to making future payments on time."

### Script 3: The Debt Settlement Negotiation

**Opening**: "I'm facing financial hardship and unable to repay the full amount. I'd like to propose a settlement."

**Request**: "I'm offering a specific settlement amount, which is a reasonable compromise considering my financial situation."

**Closing**: "I'm prepared to discuss payment terms and commit to fulfilling the agreement."

### Important Note

Remember, these scripts are templates and may need adaptation to your specific situation. Always be polite and respectful during your conversation.

### Additional Tips

**Practice Makes Perfect**: Rehearse your script beforehand to ensure clear and confident delivery.

**Be Prepared to Answer the Call**: Be ready to answer questions about your financial situation.

**Know Your Bottom Line**: Decide on your minimum acceptable outcome and be willing to walk away if necessary.

### Case Study: Mark's Negotiation Mastery

Mark, a teacher, used clear communication and a sample script as a guide to negotiate a lower interest rate with his credit card company. By following the negotiation tips, Mark successfully secured a more favorable interest rate.

### Conclusion

By using sample scripts and following the negotiation tips outlined in this chapter, you can approach your conversation with confidence and increase your chances of a successful outcome, just like Mark. Clear communication and preparation are key to achieving a favorable result.

## Putting Your Skills into Action

With your negotiation skills honed, it's time to prepare for battle. In the next chapter, we'll discuss how to gear up for a successful negotiation and launch your attack on your debt. Get ready to take control of your finances and emerge victorious!

# Part 3
# Prepare for Battle: Launching the Attack

# Chapter 6
# Gear Up for Liftoff

**Building Your Negotiation Toolkit**

Before launching into negotiation with your credit card company, it's crucial to equip yourself with the necessary tools and knowledge. By setting a clear goal, understanding your rights, practicing your pitch, and gathering evidence, you'll be well-prepared to tackle the conversation with confidence. In this chapter, we'll explore each of these essential steps to help you gear up for a successful negotiation.

**Setting a Clear Goal**

Define your desired outcome from the negotiation. What do you hope to achieve? Do you want to:

Reduce your interest rate?

Waive late fees or penalties?

Temporary payment reduction or hardship program?

Settle the debt for a lump sum?

Prioritize your goals based on your individual financial situation. If you're struggling to make payments, a temporary payment reduction or hardship program may be the most pressing concern. If you're looking to save money in the long run, a lower interest rate may be the way to go.

**Know Your Rights**

The Fair Debt Collection Practices Act (FDCPA) protects you from harassment, abuse, and unfair practices by debt collectors. Understand your rights, including:

The right to be treated with respect and dignity

The right to dispute the debt or request validation

The right to request debt verification

The right to request credit reporting corrections

Familiarize yourself with the FDCPA to confidently navigate the negotiation process.

**Practice Your Pitch**

Craft a clear and concise explanation of your financial hardship and proposed solution. Anticipate questions and objections from the credit card representative and prepare responses accordingly. Consider the following tips:

Stay calm and composed

Avoid apologetic or aggressive tone

Focus on your goal and supporting evidence

Be open to compromise and alternative solutions

**Gather Your Evidence**

Collect supporting documentation to substantiate your financial hardship and proposed solution. This may include:

Proof of income reduction or job loss

Unexpected expenses (medical bills, car repairs, etc.)

Bank statements or budget plans

Letters from creditors or collection agencies

Proof of payment history and on-time payments

Document all communication with creditors, including dates, times, and details of conversations.

**Case Study: Jessica's Just Cause**

Jessica, a waitress, lost her job due to a restaurant closure. Anticipating difficulty making her credit card payments, she decided to be proactive. Jessica researched the Fair Debt Collection Practices Act to understand her rights and gathered documentation of her job loss. Armed with this knowledge and evidence, she felt more confident approaching her credit card issuer.

**Additional Tips**

Be prepared to negotiate with a supervisor or someone with more authority

Don't be afraid to walk away if the negotiation doesn't go in your favor

Follow up with a letter or email to confirm any agreements or promises made during the negotiation

### Initiate Contact

Now that you're prepared for negotiation, it's time to take flight and contact your credit card company. By being prepared and knowledgeable, you'll be empowered to take control of your debt and negotiate a favorable outcome.

### The Negotiation Begins

In the next chapter, we'll explore the best strategies for reaching the right people and effectively communicating your situation. Get ready to take the first step towards financial freedom!

# Chapter 7
# Taking Flight: Contacting Your Credit Card Company

## Launching Your Debt-Reduction Mission

You've prepared for battle, and now it's time to take flight and contact your credit card company. Navigating the communication channels can be daunting, but with the right strategy, you'll reach the right people and set the stage for a successful negotiation.

**Choosing Your Weapon**

Decide on the most effective communication method for your situation. Phone calls and written letters both have their advantages. Phone calls offer immediate interaction and the ability to address questions and concerns on the spot. Written letters provide a paper trail and allow you to articulate your thoughts clearly.

Before making a phone call, prepare by:

Gathering all necessary documents, like your credit card

statement and proof of income

Writing down your goals and the points you want to cover

Practicing your explanation to stay focused and confident

On the other hand, written letters provide a paper trail and allow you to articulate your thoughts clearly. Consider sending a certified letter with return receipt requested to ensure receipt.

**Targeting the Right Enemy**

Find the appropriate department to reach within your credit card company. The debt settlement or hardship programs department will likely be your best bet. You can find this information on the credit card company's website or by calling their customer service number.

**Maintaining Your Armor**

Remain polite yet firm throughout the conversation. Avoid apologetic or aggressive tones, as they can undermine your position. Stay focused on your goal and remember that the representative is there to assist you.

Use phrases like:

"I appreciate your help in this matter."

"I'm looking for a solution that works for both of us."

"I'm willing to work together to find a mutually beneficial agreement."

## Telling Your Story

Clearly explain your financial hardship and the reason for your debt. Be honest and concise, providing supporting documentation if necessary. Highlight any temporary circumstances, such as a job loss or medical emergency, that have contributed to your financial struggles.

For example:

"I recently lost my job due to company restructuring and am struggling to make payments."

"I've been facing unexpected medical expenses and need

temporary assistance."

### Case Study: Brian's Best Bet

Brian, a mechanic, owed a significant amount on a single credit card. After researching his options, Brian decided a phone call would be the most efficient way to reach the hardship department of his credit card company. He practiced his explanation beforehand, focusing on the temporary nature of his financial hardship due to a recent injury. Brian remained polite and firm throughout the conversation, confidently presenting his situation and request for assistance.

### Conclusion

By choosing the right communication method, targeting the appropriate department, maintaining a professional demeanor, and clearly explaining your situation, you'll set the stage for a successful negotiation, just like Brian did by contacting the hardship department. Confidently present your case and request assistance, paving the way for a win-win outcome.

**Tools for a Win-Win Outcome**

With your communication strategy in place, it's time to enter the negotiation arena and strike a deal. In the next chapter, we'll discuss tactics for negotiating a favorable outcome and securing a win-win situation. Get ready to emerge victorious and take control of your debt!

# CHAPTER 8
# STRIKING A DEAL: THE NEGOTIATION ARENA

## Securing a Win-Win Solution

You've made it to the negotiation arena, where you'll face off with your credit card issuer to secure a favorable outcome. This is your chance to negotiate a lower interest rate, waived fees, or a debt settlement agreement. Remember, the goal is to achieve a win-win situation that benefits both you and the credit card company.

## Strategies for Victory

When negotiating with your credit card issuer, keep the following strategies in mind:

Be respectful and professional

Explain your financial situation and provide supporting documentation

Be clear about what you want to achieve

Be open to compromise

Don't be afraid to walk away if the negotiation doesn't go in your favor

For example, you could say:

"Hello, I'm having trouble making my payments due to [briefly explain your financial situation]. I'm looking for a temporary reduction in my interest rate to [specific percentage] or a waiver of my fees. Can we discuss possible options?"

**Debt Settlement as a Last Resort**

If you're unable to negotiate a favorable outcome, a debt settlement agreement may be an option. This involves paying a lump sum that's less than the full amount owed. However, this should be considered a last resort, as it can negatively impact your credit score.

Before pursuing debt settlement, consider the following:

The potential impact on your credit score

The total cost of the settlement, including any fees

Alternative options, like credit counseling or debt management plans

**Evaluating the Counter-Offer**

When the credit card company presents a counteroffer, carefully analyze it to ensure it aligns with your budget and goals. Consider the following:

Is the interest rate or fee waiver favorable?

Is the payment plan manageable?

Are there any hidden fees or penalties?

Does the agreement align with your long-term goals?

Use a checklist to ensure you don't miss any important details:

Interest rate reduction: _____

Fee waiver: _____

Payment plan: _____

Hidden fees or penalties: _____

Alignment with long-term goals: _____

**Securing Your Win**

Once you've negotiated a favorable agreement, ensure you understand the terms and conditions. Make sure the agreement is in writing and includes the following:

The reduced interest rate or waived fees

The payment plan, including the amount and frequency of payments

Any penalties or fees associated with late payments

The deadline for completing the payment plan

Monitor your progress and make adjustments as needed. Consider setting up automatic payments to ensure you never miss a payment.

### Case Study: Angela's Art of Negotiation

Angela, a freelance artist, experienced fluctuating income. She contacted her credit card company and negotiated a lower interest rate and a temporary suspension of her minimum payment due to her financial situation. Angela carefully considered the counteroffer from the credit card company, ensuring it aligned with her budget before accepting.

### Negotiate Your Way to Freedom

By employing the strategies outlined in this chapter, you can negotiate a favorable outcome with your credit card issuer, paving the way for a debt-free future. Remember to stay focused, persistent, and professional throughout the negotiation process. Strive for a win-win situation that benefits both you and the credit card company, like Angela achieved through negotiation.

### Conquering Debt Collectors

Congratulations on securing a deal! Now it's essential to understand how to manage debt collectors and avoid potential pitfalls. In the next chapter, we'll explore strategies for facing debt collectors and maintaining control. Get ready to take the next step towards financial freedom!

# Chapter 9
# Facing the Debt Collectors

**Your Rights, Your Money**

Dealing with debt collectors can be intimidating, but it's essential to know your rights and how to manage their requests. In this chapter, we'll explore strategies for communicating with debt collectors, understanding your rights under the Fair Debt Collection Practices Act, and negotiating payment plans. We'll also discuss debt relief options, including debt management plans and debt settlement.

**Knowing Your Rights**

The Fair Debt Collection Practices Act (FDCPA) protects consumers from harassing and abusive debt collection practices. Understand your rights under the FDCPA:

Debt collectors cannot harass or abuse you

Debt collectors cannot lie or misrepresent themselves

Debt collectors must validate the debt upon request

For example, debt collectors cannot:

Debt collectors must respect your request to stop contacting you

Call you repeatedly or use abusive language

Claim to be law enforcement or a government agency

Threaten to arrest you or seize your assets

Refuse to provide their name or company information

**Defending Yourself**

Identify and respond to harassing or abusive collection tactics:

Keep a record of all communication with debt collectors, including dates, times, and details of conversations

Report any violations of the FDCPA to the Federal Trade Commission (FTC) or your state Attorney General's office

Send a cease and desist letter to stop unwanted contact

**Here's an example of a cease and desist letter:**

[Your Name]

[Your Address]

[City, State, ZIP]

[Date]

[Debt Collector's Name]

[Debt Collector's Company]

[Debt Collector's Address]

[City, State, ZIP]

Dear [Debt Collector's Name],

I am writing to request that you immediately stop contacting me regarding the alleged debt. Your collection tactics have been harassing and abusive, and I will not tolerate further communication.

Please confirm in writing that you have received this request and will cease all contact.

[Your Name]

## Verifying the Debt

Request verification of the debt and any outstanding balance from the collector:

Request proof of the debt and your responsibility for it

Verify the amount and any interest or fees

Ensure the debt is not past the statute of limitations

## Case Study: Maria's Debt Validation

Maria, a freelance writer, received a collection letter from a debt collector claiming she owed $1,500 on a credit card account. Maria was skeptical, as she had never received any statements or notifications from the credit card company. She requested debt validation from the collector, including proof of the debt and her responsibility for it. The collector failed to provide any evidence, and Maria disputed the debt. The collector eventually closed the account, and Maria avoided paying a debt she didn't owe.

**Here's an example of a debt verification letter:**

[Your Name]

[Your Address]

[City, State, ZIP]

[Date]

[Debt Collector's Name]

[Debt Collector's Company]

[Debt Collector's Address]

[City, State, ZIP]

Dear [Debt Collector's Name],

I am writing to request verification of the alleged debt. Please provide proof of the debt, including the original contract or agreement, and any outstanding balance.

Additionally, please confirm that the debt is not past the statute of limitations in my state.

Sincerely,

[Your Name]

## Negotiating Directly

If applicable, negotiate a payment plan directly with the debt collector (if they represent the original creditor):

Explain your financial situation and propose a payment plan

Request a temporary reduction in payments or interest

Ensure any agreement is in writing and includes all terms

## Case Study: John's Payment Plan

John, a small business owner, fell behind on his credit card payments due to a slow period in his business. He contacted the credit card company and negotiated a payment plan to pay off the outstanding balance over six months. John made timely payments and communicated regularly with the credit card company, which agreed to waive late fees and reduce the interest rate. John successfully paid off the debt and avoided further damage to his credit score.

**Here's an example of a payment plan agreement:**

[Your Name]

[Your Address]

[City, State, ZIP]

[Date]

[Debt Collector's Name]

[Debt Collector's Company]

[Debt Collector's Address]

[City, State, ZIP]

Payment Plan Agreement

I, [Your Name], agree to pay [Debt Collector's Company] the sum of $[Amount] per month for [Number] months, starting on [Date], to settle the outstanding debt of $[Amount].

This payment plan is contingent on the following terms:

The debt collector will not report any late payments to the credit bureaus during the payment plan period.

The debt collector will waive any late fees or penalties.

The debt collector will provide a written confirmation of the payment plan and any changes to the original debt amount.

By signing below, both parties acknowledge acceptance of this payment plan agreement.

[Your Signature]

[Debt Collector's Signature]

[Date]

## Debt Relief Options

### Debt Management Plan (DMP)

A structured repayment plan created by a credit counseling agency that allows you to consolidate your debts into one monthly payment with potentially lower interest rates and waived fees. You still repay the full amount owed.

Impact on Credit Score: Enrolling in a DMP may cause a temporary dip in your credit score due to inquiries and potential account closures. However, making consistent on-time payments through the program can significantly improve your score in the long run.

### Debt Settlement

An agreement with a debt settlement company to negotiate a lump-sum payment with your creditors to settle your debt for less than the total owed. This negatively impacts your credit score and can take several years to complete.

Impact on Credit Score: Debt settlement typically has a more severe and long-lasting negative impact on your credit score compared to a DMP. Since you're not repaying the full amount owed, it will be marked as a settled account on your credit report, which can stay there for seven years.

### Case Study: Emily's Debt Settlement

Emily, a student, accumulated significant credit card debt while in college. She struggled to make payments and eventually stopped paying altogether. Emily contacted a debt settlement company, which negotiated a lump-sum payment with her creditors to settle the debt for less than the total owed. Emily made the payment and avoided further collection activity, but her credit score was negatively impacted due to the settled account.

### Knowledge is Power

By asserting your rights and understanding the legalities, you can effectively manage communication with debt collectors, just like Carlos. Remember, knowledge is power, and being prepared will help you stay in control of your debt repayment journey.

### Building Your Budget and Crushing Debt

With debt collectors managed, you're ready to build momentum and stick to your plan. In the next part, we'll discuss how to create a budget, prioritize debt repayment, and stay motivated throughout your debt-slaying journey. Get ready to take the next step towards financial freedom!

# Part 4
# Slay the Dragon: Sticking to Your Repayment Plan

# Chapter 10
# Building Momentum: Crafting Your Budget Weapon

## Creating Your Winning Budget

Welcome to the next stage of your debt-slaying journey! In this chapter, we'll explore the crucial steps to create a winning budget strategy that will help you conquer your debt and achieve financial freedom. A well-crafted budget is your most powerful weapon in the battle against debt, and we'll show you how to forge it.

**Forge Your Budget**

Creating a realistic budget is the first step towards financial freedom. It's essential to track your income and expenses to understand where your money is going. Start by:

Identifying your income from all sources

Listing your fixed expenses, such as rent/mortgage, utilities, and groceries

Accounting for variable expenses, like entertainment and travel

Setting financial goals, like debt repayment and savings targets

**Use the following template to track your income and expenses:**

| Income Source | Amount |
|---|---|
| Salary | $_____ |
| Investments | $_____ |
| Other | $_____ |
| Total Income | $_____ |

| Expense Category | Amount |
|---|---|
| Rent/Mortgage | $_____ |
| Utilities | $_____ |
| Groceries | $_____ |
| Transportation | $_____ |
| Entertainment | |

| Income Source | Amount |
|---|---|
| | $_____ |

| Income Source | Amount |
|---|---|
| Debt Repayment | $_____ |

| Income Source | Amount |
|---|---|
| Savings | $_____ |
| Total Expenses | $_____ |

## Identify Your Weaknesses

Once you have a clear picture of your finances, it's time to identify areas where you can cut back on unnecessary spending. Common weaknesses include:

Dining out too frequently

Subscription services you don't use

Impulse purchases

To overcome these weaknesses, try:

Cooking at home instead of dining out

Canceling subscription services you don't use

Implementing a 30-day waiting period before making impulse purchases

## Prioritize Your Targets

Now it's time to focus on paying down debt using one of two strategies: the Debt Avalanche or Debt Snowball method.

## Debt Avalanche

This method prioritizes paying off debts with the highest interest rates first, saving you the most money on interest in the long run.

List your debts from highest interest rate to lowest

Make minimum payments on all debts except the one with the highest interest rate

Put all extra money towards paying down the debt with the highest interest rate

Repeat the process until all debts are paid off

## Debt Snowball

This method prioritizes paying off the smallest debts first, regardless of interest rate, providing a motivational boost as you quickly eliminate debts.

List your debts from smallest balance to largest

Make minimum payments on all debts except the one with the smallest balance

Put all extra money towards paying down the debt with the smallest balance

Repeat the process until all debts are paid off

**Enlist Technological Allies**

Utilize budgeting tools and apps to stay on track and monitor your progress. Some popular options include:

Mint

Personal Capital

YNAB (You Need a Budget)

Each tool offers unique features and benefits, so it's essential to choose the one that best fits your needs. You will find links to each in the Appendix.

**Case Study: David's Diligently Crafted Budget**

David, a recent college graduate, struggled to manage his credit card debt. By tracking his spending for a month, he realized he was spending more on dining out than he thought. David adjusted his budget, allocating more funds towards debt payments and reducing his eating-out expenses.

## The Keys to Debt Slaying Success

A well-crafted budget, combined with a strategic approach to prioritizing your debt payments, is your key weapon in gaining momentum and slaying the debt dragon for good, just like David. Stay motivated and focused on your goals, and you'll be debt-free in no time!

## Strategies for Maintaining Momentum

Now that you've built momentum in your debt repayment journey, it's essential to stay motivated and focused on your goals. In the next chapter, we'll explore strategies for maintaining your momentum and keep your goals in sight.

# Chapter 11
# Fan the Flames of Motivation

**Fueling Your Motivation for Debt-Free Victory**

Congratulations on making it this far in your debt-slaying journey! You've taken the first crucial steps towards financial freedom, and now it's time to maintain focus and determination to achieve debt-free victory. In this chapter, we'll explore the strategies to keep you motivated and inspired throughout your journey.

**Track Your Victories**

Monitoring your progress and celebrating milestones is essential to staying inspired. Visualize your progress with charts or graphs that illustrate your debt reduction. For example, you can use a debt repayment tracker template to chart your progress.

| Month | Debt Balance | Payment | Progress |
| --- | --- | --- | --- |
| January | $10,000 | $500 | 5% |
| February | $9,500 | $500 | 10% |
| March | $9,000 | $500 | 15% |

Reward yourself for achieving small goals along the way, like completing a month of on-time payments or paying off a specific debt. Treat yourself to a non-debt-related purchase, like a new book or a fun activity.

**Set SMART Goals**

Establish short-term and long-term goals to visualize your success. Short-term goals focus on milestones within a few weeks or months, like reducing your credit card spending by a certain amount or saving a specific amount for a debt payment.

| Goal | Amount | Deadline |
|---|---|---|
| Reduce credit card spending | $500 | 3 months |
| Save for debt payment | $1,000 | 6 months |

Long-term goals envision your future financial freedom, like becoming debt-free within a specific timeframe or building a healthy emergency fund.

| Goal | Amount | Deadline |
|---|---|---|
| Become debt-free | $0 | 12 months |
| Build emergency fund | $5,000 | 18 months |

### Reward Yourself Wisely

Celebrate achievements along the way with non-financial rewards. Try a new hobby, spend quality time with loved ones, or plan a fun activity.

| Reward | Cost | Deadline |
|---|---|---|
| Try a new hobby | $0 | 1 month |
| Spend quality time with loved ones | $0 | 2 months |
| Plan a fun activity | $0 | 3 months |

**Find Your Support System**

Share your goals with a trusted friend or family member for accountability. Join a support group, like a local financial counseling service or online forum, to connect with others on a similar journey.

| Support System | Contact | Deadline |
| --- | --- | --- |
| Friend | Monthly check-ins | Ongoing |
| Support group | Bi-weekly meetings | Ongoing |

By implementing these strategies, you'll stay motivated and focused on your goals, just like Lisa, Michael, Brian, and Sarah.

## Building Your Motivation Arsenal

Staying motivated is essential for slaying the debt dragon and reaching your debt-free future. By employing strategies like tracking progress, setting SMART goals, rewarding yourself wisely, and finding a support system, you can keep the flames of motivation burning brightly.

## Securing Your Financial Future

With motivation and focus in place, you're ready to tackle the final stretch of your debt repayment journey. In the next part, we'll explore the essential steps to take after achieving debt freedom, including rebuilding your credit and developing sustainable financial habits.

# Part 5
# Fortify Your Finances: Building a Secure Future

# Chapter 12: Rebuild Your Credit Walls

## Understanding the Rules for Financial Success

Congratulations on defeating the debt dragon! Now it's time to strengthen your credit score and build a secure financial future. In this chapter, we'll explore the importance of understanding credit scoring, making timely payments, maintaining low credit utilization, considering secured credit cards, and disputing errors on your credit report.

## Understanding the Credit Score Arena

Your credit score is a three-digit number that represents your creditworthiness. The most widely used credit score is the FICO score, which ranges from 300 to 850. The three major credit bureaus, Equifax, Experian, and TransUnion, each have slightly different scores for you. Your credit score is influenced by five factors: payment history (most important), credit utilization ratio, credit mix, length of credit history, and new credit inquiries.

## Make Timely Payments

Consistently pay all future credit card bills on time and in full. On-time payments are the most significant factor influencing your credit score. Set up automatic payments and reminders to ensure you never miss a payment.

### Maintain Low Credit Utilization

Keep your credit card balances low, ideally below 30% of your credit limit. This demonstrates responsible credit card usage to potential lenders. Calculate your credit utilization ratio by dividing your credit card balance by your credit limit. For example, if your credit limit is $1,000 and your balance is $300, your credit utilization ratio is 30%.

### Consider Secured Credit Cards

Explore using a secured credit card to rebuild your credit history if necessary. Secured credit cards require a security deposit that becomes your credit limit. Using a secured card responsibly and making on-time payments can positively impact your score. Choose a secured credit card with no annual fee and a low interest rate.

### Dispute Errors

Challenge any inaccuracies on your credit report to ensure its accuracy. Obtain a free credit report from each credit bureau and review it for errors. Dispute errors directly with the credit bureau that reported them. Keep detailed records of your disputes and follow up until they are resolved.

### Building a Solid Financial Foundation

By following these steps and maintaining good credit habits, you can rebuild your credit walls and achieve a strong financial standing, just like David, Angela, Lisa, Brian, and Sarah.

### Habits for Long-Term Security

Now that you've taken steps to rebuild your credit, it's crucial to maintain good credit habits and avoid falling into debt traps again. In the next chapter, we'll discuss the importance of living within your means and developing sustainable financial habits for long-term financial security.

# Chapter 13
# Live Within Your Means: The Long-Term Defense

**Tools for Lasting Financial Freedom**

Congratulations on conquering the debt dragon! Now it's time to develop sustainable financial habits to avoid future debt traps and build a secure financial future. In this chapter, we'll explore the importance of creating a sustainable budget, prioritizing needs over wants, choosing wise spending tools, building an emergency fund, and seeking professional help when needed.

**Create a Sustainable Budget**

Craft a budget that allocates funds for savings and unexpected expenses. Revisit and update your budget regularly to reflect changes in income or expenses. Use the following template to create a budget that works for you:

| Category | Monthly Allocation |
| --- | --- |
| Housing | $1,500 |
| Food | $500 |
| Utilities | $150 |
| Transportation | $200 |
| Insurance | $100 |
| Savings | $500 |
| Emergency Fund | $500 |
| Entertainment | $200 |

### Case Study: David's Dynamic Budget

David, from previous chapters, realized his budget needed flexibility. He added a buffer category for unexpected expenses and adjusted allocations as his income increased, allowing him to save more towards his goals.

### Prioritize Needs Over Wants

Focus on essential expenses and avoid impulse purchases. Distinguish between needs (essentials for survival) and wants (desires that can be postponed). Use the following categories to prioritize your expenses:

| **Needs** | **Wants** |
|---|---|
| Housing | Dining out |
| Food | Entertainment |
| Utilities | Hobbies |
| Transportation | Travel |
| Insurance | Clothing |

### Case Study: Angela's Needs vs. Wants

Angela, from Chapter 8, prioritized essentials like housing and groceries after conquering her debt. She implemented a "wait 24 hours" rule, curbing impulse spending.

### Choose Wise Spending Tools

Consider using debit cards or cash to manage your spending and avoid credit card debt. Debit cards deduct funds directly from your checking account, promoting mindful spending. Using cash creates a physical barrier between you and impulsive purchases.

### Case Study: Lisa's Cash is King Approach

Lisa, from Chapter 3, switched to cash for everyday purchases after overcoming debt struggles. This tangible representation of her spending helped her stay within her budget.

### Build an Emergency Fund

Create a safety net by establishing an emergency fund to cover unexpected costs and prevent reliance on credit. Aim to save 3-6 months' worth of living expenses in your emergency fund. Consider opening a dedicated savings account with a higher interest rate than your checking account.

**Case Study: Brian's Buffer Builder**

Brian, from Chapter 7, prioritized building an emergency fund after negotiating a debt settlement. He started small and gradually built a safety net.

**Seek Professional Help**

Consider consulting a financial advisor for personalized guidance on managing your finances and achieving your long-term goals. Find a financial advisor or credit counselor in your area through the National Association of Personal Financial Advisors (NAPFA) or the National Foundation for Credit Counseling (NFCC).

By following these strategies and learning from the success stories of David, Angela, Lisa, Brian, and Sarah, you can build a secure financial future and achieve lasting financial freedom.

### Case Study: Sarah's Smart Seeking

Sarah, from Chapter 1, consulted a financial advisor after overcoming debt. The advisor helped her create a customized budget, investment strategy, and plan for long-term financial security.

### Practical Steps to a Secure Future

Living within your means and practicing responsible financial habits will ensure a long-term, secure financial fortress. By following these strategies and learning from the success stories of David, Angela, Lisa, Brian, and Sarah, you can build a secure financial future and achieve lasting financial freedom.

### Debt-Free and Thriving

Congratulations on achieving debt freedom! By following

the principles outlined in this book, you'll be well on your way to a brighter financial future. Remember, financial freedom is a journey, and living within your means is the key to long-term success.

# Conclusion
# Your Financial Freedom Starts Now

Congratulations on reaching the final chapter of your debt-slaying journey! As you close this book, remember that the strategies and stories shared within its pages are not just words on paper – they are the keys to unlocking a life free from the shackles of credit card debt.

**Summary**

Let's recap the key takeaways from our journey together:

Face your debt head-on and take responsibility for your financial future.

Create a budget that works for you, not against you.

Prioritize your debts and tackle them one by one.

Use the snowball method or avalanche method to stay focused and motivated.

Negotiate with creditors and consider debt consolidation or settlement.

Rebuild your credit and maintain good credit habits.

Develop sustainable financial habits to avoid future debt traps.

**Encouragement**

By reading this book, you've taken the first step towards debt freedom – and that's something to be proud of! You've shown that you're willing to confront your debt and take control of your financial future. Remember, debt freedom is within your reach, and every small step you take gets you closer to your goal.

**Final Thoughts**

**"Believe you can and you're halfway there." – Theodore Roosevelt**

Staying motivated and committed to your debt-slaying journey is crucial. Remember why you started this journey in the first place – to break free from the stress and anxiety of debt and build a brighter financial future. Keep your eyes on the prize and celebrate your small victories along the way.

### Call to Action

As you achieve debt freedom, don't be silent about your success! Share your story with others and inspire them to take control of their debt. Your journey can be a beacon of hope for those struggling in the darkness of debt. Share your triumphs and encourage others to join you on the path to financial freedom.

In conclusion, remember that debt freedom is not just a destination – it's a journey. Stay committed, stay motivated, and most importantly, stay proud of yourself for taking control of your financial future. You got this!

### Final Words

As you close this book, remember that you're not alone in your debt-slaying journey. There are countless others who have walked in your shoes and have emerged victorious on the other side. You can do the same. Keep pushing forward, and know that a life free from credit card debt is waiting for you on the other side.

Thank you for joining me on this journey. I'm honored to have been a part of your debt-slaying journey, and I can't wait to hear about your success stories. Keep shining, and remember – debt freedom is just the beginning!

# Appendix
# Resources for Financial Empowerment

Congratulations on taking the first step towards financial freedom! In this appendix, we've compiled a list of resources to help you continue your journey towards financial empowerment.

**Government Agencies**

Consumer Financial Protection Bureau (CFPB): The CFPB is a government agency dedicated to protecting consumers from unfair and deceptive financial practices. Their website offers a wealth of financial education and resources, including guides on managing debt, understanding credit scores, and avoiding financial scams. https://www.consumerfinance.gov/

Federal Trade Commission (FTC): The FTC is responsible for enforcing federal laws related to consumer protection and unfair competition. Their website provides information on managing debt, credit, and personal finance, as well as resources for reporting fraud and scams. https://www.ftc.gov/

Internal Revenue Service (IRS): The IRS offers resources on tax credits, deductions, and other tax-related topics on their website. https://www.irs.gov/

**Non-Profit Organizations**

National Foundation for Credit Counseling (NFCC): The NFCC is a non-profit organization that provides credit counseling and debt management services to consumers. Their website offers a directory of member agencies and resources for managing debt. https://www.nfcc.org/

Financial Counseling Association of America (FCAA): The FCAA is a non-profit organization that provides credit counseling and debt management services to consumers. Their website offers resources on budgeting, credit, and debt management. https://fcaa.org/

National Association of Consumer Advocates (NACA): NACA is a non-profit organization that provides resources and support for consumers facing financial difficulties. Their website offers information on credit, debt, and consumer protection. https://www.consumeradvocates.org/

## Online Tools and Apps

Mint: Mint is a personal finance app that allows you to track your spending, create a budget, and set financial goals.
https://mint.intuit.com/

Personal Capital: Personal Capital is a financial management app that allows you to track your income and expenses, investments, and debts.
https://home.personalcapital.com/page/login/goHome

Credit Karma: Credit Karma is a credit monitoring service that provides free credit scores and reports from TransUnion.
https://www.creditkarma.com/auth/logon

NerdWallet: NerdWallet is a personal finance website that offers resources on budgeting, credit, and investing.
https://www.nerdwallet.com/

The Balance: The Balance is a personal finance website that offers resources on budgeting, credit, and debt management.
https://www.thebalancemoney.com/

## Additional Resources

AnnualCreditReport.com: This website provides free credit reports from all three major credit reporting agencies (Experian, TransUnion, and Equifax). https://www.annualcreditreport.com/index.action

Experian: This website provides free credit scores and reports from Experian. https://www.experian.com/

Debtors Anonymous: This website provides resources and support for individuals struggling with debt addiction. https://debtorsanonymous.org/

Remember, financial empowerment is within your reach. Take advantage of these resources to continue your journey towards financial freedom.

**Final Thoughts**

Managing your finances and overcoming debt takes time, effort, and patience. But with the right resources and support, you can achieve financial freedom and build a brighter financial future. Don't be afraid to reach out for help when you need it, and remember to stay committed to your financial goals.

www.ingramcontent.com/pod-product-compliance
Lightning Source LLC
Chambersburg PA
CBHW071941210526
45479CB00002B/772